weird but true!

The opening text crawl in the STAR WARS films was inspired by popular adventure and superhero film serials from the 1930s.

NATIONAL
GEOGRAPHIC

weird but true!

STAR WARS

300 EPIC FACTS
FROM A GALAXY FAR,
FAR AWAY....

NATIONAL GEOGRAPHIC
WASHINGTON, D.C.

THE FIRST SCENE IN EVERY FILM IN THE SKYWALKER SAGA TAKES PLACE IN SPACE.

4

SEVENTY-THREE DIFFERENT ALIEN SPECIES APPEAR IN THE ORIGINAL TRILOGY FILMS.

THE **GRILLE** ON **REY'S SPEEDER**
IN *STAR WARS: THE FORCE AWAKENS* WAS INSPIRED BY
SPORTS CARS FROM THE 1920s.

That's weird!

Ewok makeup designers looked at the faces of Brussels griffon dogs for inspiration.

8

The actor who
was the voice of

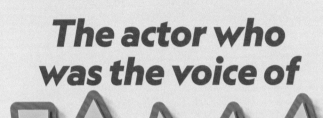

in the Toy Story films
played a rebel officer in
Star Wars: The Empire
Strikes Back.

Luke Skywalker's name was originally **LUKE STARKILLER,** but **George Lucas,** the creator of *Star Wars,* changed it on the **FIRST DAY OF FILMING.**

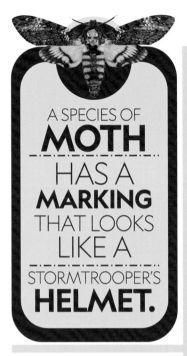

A SPECIES OF **MOTH** HAS A **MARKING** THAT LOOKS LIKE A STORMTROOPER'S **HELMET.**

GEORGE LUCAS ORIGINALLY OFFERED THE ROLE OF **YODA** TO MUPPETS CREATOR **JIM** HENSON.

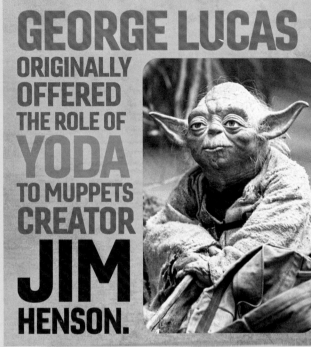

Crew members used stepladders to **reach** the tops of **actors** in **costume** as Wookiees.

Actors for the video game *Star Wars: Battlefront II* wore motion capture suits with sensors all over their **bodies to record their movements.**

That's weird!

THE **DAGOBAH SET** WAS SO **LARGE** THAT IT INCLUDED **A REAL RUNNING RIVER.**

ANIMALS BROUGHT TO THE SET INCLUDED **PYTHONS,** AN **ANACONDA,** AND **IGUANAS.**

13

A CIRCUS PERFORMER PLAYED THE FOUR-ARMED ARDENNIAN PILOT RIO DURANT ON SET IN THE FILM *SOLO: A STAR WARS STORY.*

World War II fighter planes inspired the design of **REBEL SHIPS** in the **STAR WARS GALAXY.**

IT TOOK **SIX** PUPPETEERS — FOUR OF WHOM WORKED **INSIDE** THE JABBA PUPPET — TO BRING **JABBA THE HUTT TO LIFE IN** STAR WARS: RETURN OF THE JEDI.

WARWICK DAVIS, THE ACTOR WHO PLAYED THE EWOK WICKET W. WARRICK, WAS ONLY

11 YEARS OLD
WHEN HE FILMED *RETURN OF THE JEDI.*

He returned to play **Wicket** in *Star Wars: The Rise of Skywalker,* alongside his teenage son, who played an Ewok named **Pommet.**

AT THE END OF
THE CREDITS IN
STAR WARS:
THE PHANTOM
MENACE
YOU CAN
HEAR THE
SOUND OF
DARTH
VADER
BREATHING.

17

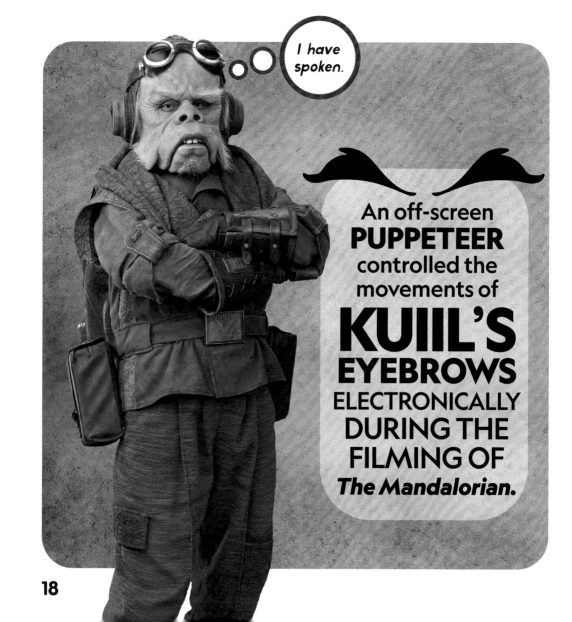

I have spoken.

An off-screen **PUPPETEER** controlled the movements of **KUIIL'S EYEBROWS** ELECTRONICALLY DURING THE FILMING OF *The Mandalorian.*

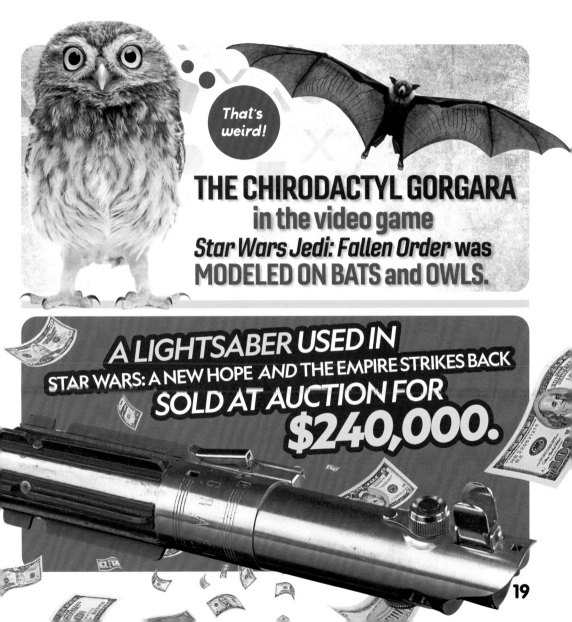

That's weird!

THE CHIRODACTYL GORGARA
in the video game
Star Wars Jedi: Fallen Order was
MODELED ON BATS and OWLS.

A LIGHTSABER USED IN *STAR WARS: A NEW HOPE AND THE EMPIRE STRIKES BACK* **SOLD AT AUCTION FOR $240,000.**

The full-scale **MILLENNIUM FALCON** built for *THE EMPIRE STRIKES BACK* weighed **25 TONS** (22.7 t)—more than an average whale shark.

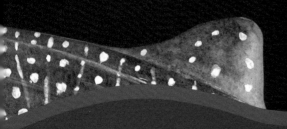

JABBA THE HUTT'S PET KOWAKIAN MONKEY-LIZARD, **SALACIOUS B. CRUMB,**

IS ONE OF ONLY TWO *STAR WARS* CHARACTERS

TO PROMINENTLY **DISPLAY** A MIDDLE INITIAL. (THE OTHER IS WICKET W. WARRICK.)

The director of *Star Wars: The Last Jedi* **PLAYED** a Death Star **GUNNER** in *Rogue One: A Star Wars Story.*

The director of Rogue One played a Resistance fighter in The Last Jedi.

That's weird!

Chewbacca's furry coat was **knitted together** from **goat** and **yak hair.**

The Wood Between the Worlds in the Chronicles of Narnia series inspired the **WORLD BETWEEN WORLDS** in *Star Wars Rebels* and *Ahsoka*.

THE INSPIRATION FOR MAZ KANATA WAS AN ENGLISH TEACHER OF THE DIRECTOR OF *THE FORCE AWAKENS*, WHO WORE LARGE GLASSES.

HARRISON FORD WAS WORKING AS A CARPENTER WHEN HE WAS CAST AS HAN SOLO IN *STAR WARS*.

24

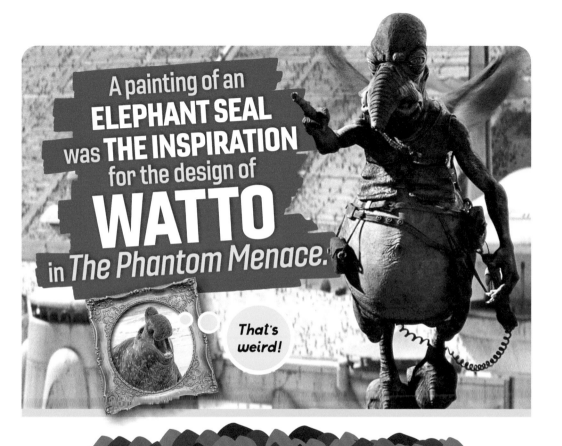

A painting of an **ELEPHANT SEAL** was **THE INSPIRATION** for the design of **WATTO** in *The Phantom Menace.*

That's weird!

George Lucas based the design of Chewbacca on his dog Indiana.

BB-8 beeps **705** times in the sequel trilogy films.

That's weird!

A FRUIT BAT FOUND IN PAPUA NEW GUINEA WAS NICKNAMED THE YODA BAT BECAUSE IT LOOKS LIKE THE JEDI MASTER.

27

Recordings of FLYING FOXES were among the sounds used to create GEONOSIAN NOISES in *STAR WARS: ATTACK OF THE CLONES.*

UNUSED PILOT FOOTAGE FROM *A NEW HOPE* CAN BE SEEN IN THE BATTLE ABOVE SCARIF IN *ROGUE ONE.*

It takes **THREE PEOPLE—AN ACTOR,** a **WEAPONS EXPERT,** and a **HAND-TO-HAND COMBAT SPECIALIST—**to **PLAY** the **MANDALORIAN.**

THE ACTOR WHO VOICED THE TITLE CHARACTER IN THE FILM *E.T. THE EXTRA-TERRESTRIAL* ALSO PERFORMED LEIA'S VOICE WHEN SHE WAS IN HER BOUSHH DISGUISE IN *RETURN OF THE JEDI.*

REY WAS ORIGINALLY NAMED KIRA.

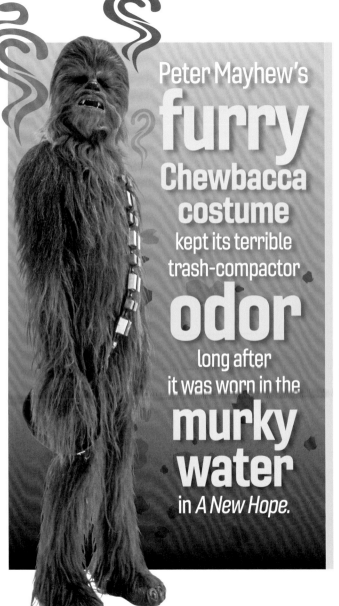

Peter Mayhew's **furry** Chewbacca costume kept its terrible trash-compactor **odor** long after it was worn in the **murky water** in *A New Hope*.

The actor who played GRAND MOFF TARKIN in *A NEW HOPE* WORE SLIPPERS during filming because the boots for his COSTUME WERE TOO TIGHT.

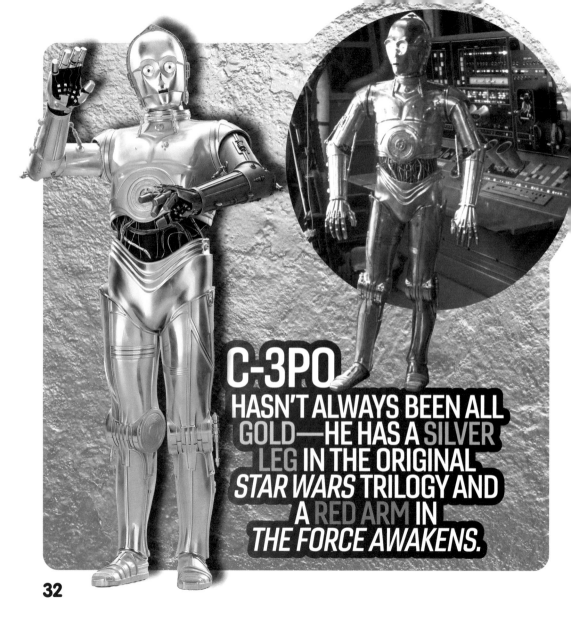

C-3PO

HASN'T ALWAYS BEEN ALL GOLD—HE HAS A SILVER LEG IN THE ORIGINAL *STAR WARS* TRILOGY AND A RED ARM IN *THE FORCE AWAKENS.*

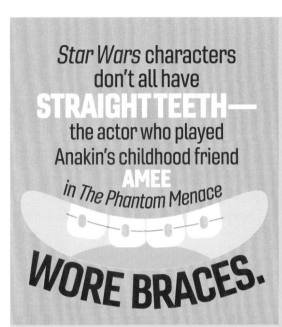

Star Wars characters don't all have **STRAIGHT TEETH**— the actor who played Anakin's childhood friend **AMEE** in *The Phantom Menace* **WORE BRACES.**

A KITCHEN SINK CAN BE SPOTTED AMONG THE SPACE DEBRIS IN THE **OPENING** SPACE **BATTLE IN** *STAR WARS: REVENGE OF THE SITH.*

Some of the **LAVA EFFECTS** in *Revenge of the Sith* came from footage of the volcano Mount Etna **ERUPTING.**

In 2022, more than **1,200** babies were named **Leia** in the United States.

34

The same year
in the
United States,
more than
400
babies
were named
Anakin.

15,000 FEATHERS were attached by hand to every **PORG** created for *THE LAST JEDI*.

Two film studios **passed on the idea** of *Star Wars* before it found a home at **20th Century FOX.**

An extinct marine **ARTHROPOD** was named after **HAN SOLO.**

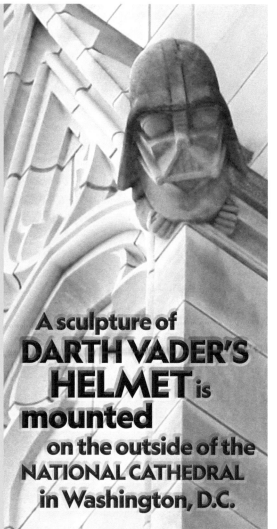

A sculpture of **DARTH VADER'S HELMET** is **mounted** on the outside of the **NATIONAL CATHEDRAL in Washington, D.C.**

37

In 2020, the Empire State Building in New York City displayed **holiday-themed** *Star Wars* characters and vehicles made out of **LEGO®** bricks in its windows.

MATT LANTER, WHO **VOICED** ANAKIN SKYWALKER IN *STAR WARS: THE CLONE WARS,* WAS TOLD HE WAS **AUDITIONING** FOR THE MADE-UP ROLE OF **"DEAK STARKILLER."**

BOBA FETT
FIRST APPEARED
IN A NORTHERN CALIFORNIA, U.S.A., PARADE
IN 1978—TWO YEARS BEFORE *THE EMPIRE STRIKES BACK*
DEBUTED IN THEATERS.

I go way back.

That's weird!

AUDIO RECORDINGS OF
BEARS,
WALRUSES,
DOLPHINS,
OTTERS,

BIRDS, AND CATS HELPED CREATE STAR WARS SOUNDS.

Purr-fect!

In the opening scene of A New Hope, the model of the **rebel ship** Tantive IV was **attached** to the **Imperial Star Destroyer** with a **paper clip.**

42

Rancho Obi-Wan, a MUSEUM in California, contains an estimated **500,000** Star Wars items in its collection.

The creature performer who played **the Frog Lady** in *The Mandalorian* could only **see** out of the mouth of **her** costume.

SPED-UP RECORDINGS of the southern African language **isiZulu** were used for **JAWAESE DIALOGUE** in **A New Hope**.

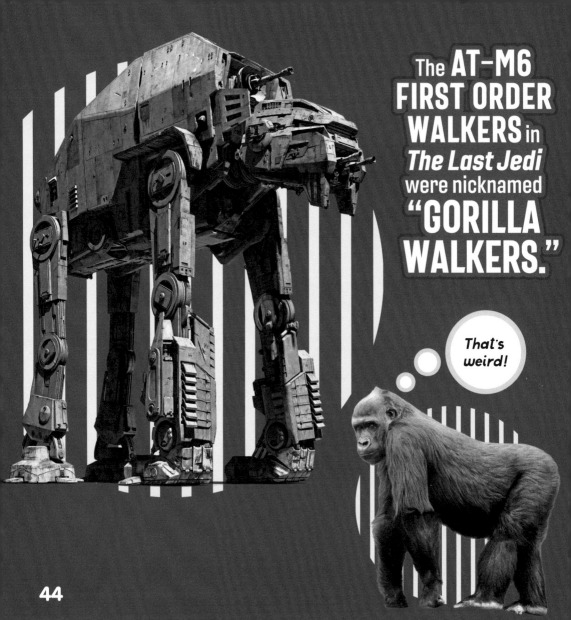

The **AT-M6 FIRST ORDER WALKERS** in *The Last Jedi* were nicknamed **"GORILLA WALKERS."**

That's weird!

44

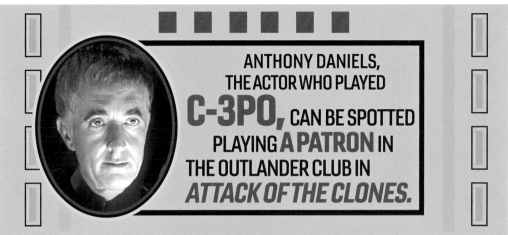

ANTHONY DANIELS, THE ACTOR WHO PLAYED **C-3PO,** CAN BE SPOTTED PLAYING **A PATRON** IN THE OUTLANDER CLUB IN *ATTACK OF THE CLONES.*

Black beans were one of the **main ingredients** used to create the **sinking field** in *The Rise of Skywalker.*

Alec Guinness, who played Jedi Master Obi-Wan Kenobi, was **KNIGHTED** BY QUEEN ELIZABETH II.

A recording of a young black bear named Pooh in Tehachapi, California, was one of the animal sounds used for Chewbacca's vocalizations.

Stormtroopers MISS THEIR TARGETS **296 TIMES** DURING THE DEATH STAR ESCAPE IN *A New Hope.*

IN EARLY STAR WARS SCRIPTS, "MAY THE FORCE BE WITH YOU" WAS "MAY THE FORCE OF OTHERS BE WITH YOU."

BEFORE THE FIRST ORDER'S **BB UNIT** WAS OFFICIALLY NAMED **BB-9E**, THE DARK DROID WAS NICKNAMED **"BB-HATE"** BY THE CREW OF *THE LAST JEDI.*

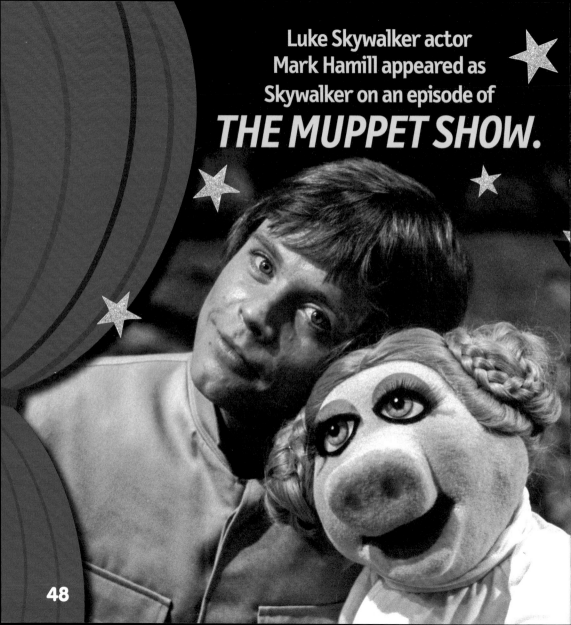

Luke Skywalker actor
Mark Hamill appeared as
Skywalker on an episode of
THE MUPPET SHOW.

48

Miss Piggy dressed up as Princess Leia.

THE SCENE OF DARTH VADER'S **FUNERAL PYRE** IN *RETURN OF THE JEDI* WAS FILMED AT **SKYWALKER RANCH** IN CALIFORNIA— THE HEADQUARTERS OF LUCASFILM AT THE TIME.

THE ACTOR WHO PLAYED R2-D2 WAS ALSO ORIGINALLY CAST AS WICKET THE EWOK.

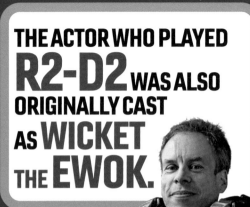

When the actor fell ill with **FOOD POISONING,** the filmmakers had Warwick Davis play Wicket—and Davis has now been part of the franchise for more than **FOUR DECADES.**

RETURN OF THE JEDI **WAS ORIGINALLY TITLED** *REVENGE OF THE JEDI.*

THE SAGA CONTINUES.

STAR WARS
REVENGE OF THE JEDI

THE NAME WAS CHANGED SO LATE THAT POSTERS **WERE MADE WITH THE *REVENGE* TITLE.**

The design process
for the U-wing ship

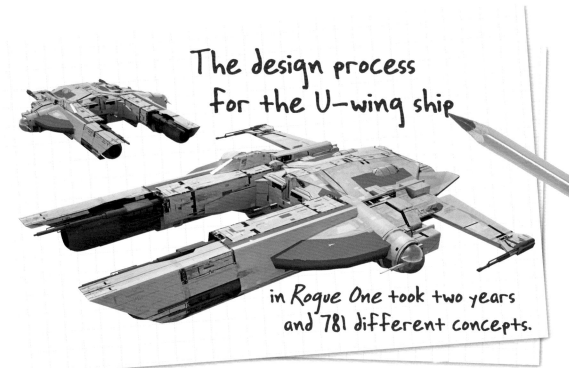

in *Rogue One* took two years
and 781 different concepts.

A VEXIS SNAKE PUPPET was used during the
filming of *The Rise of Skywalker*, but the snake
in the final film is MOSTLY COMPUTER EFFECTS.

R2-D2'S "SCREAM"

IS A SPED-UP RECORDING OF SOUND ENGINEER

BEN BURTT'S **OWN SCREAM.**

Savage Opress's armor in The Clone Wars is based on ancient Roman armor.

52

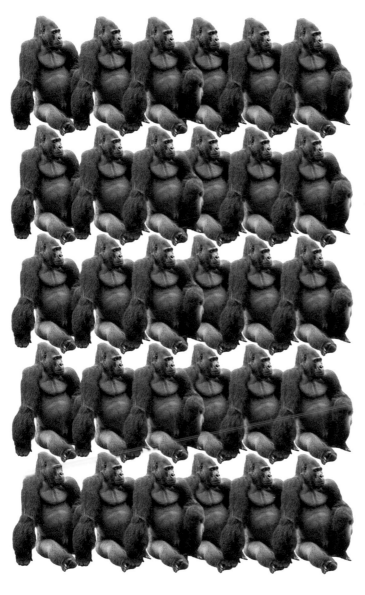

THE LAST JEDI
CREATURE DESIGNERS BUILT A MODEL OF A FATHIER THAT USED SIX TONS (5.4 T) OF WET CLAY—THE WEIGHT OF MORE THAN 30 GORILLAS.

Princess Leia's **iconic** *side buns in* A New Hope *were inspired by the* **hairstyles** *of women who fought in the* **Mexican Revolution.**

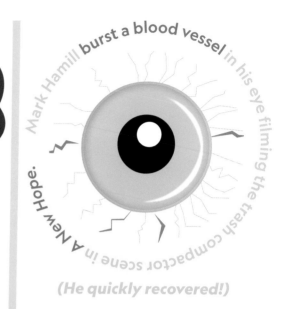

Mark Hamill burst a blood vessel in his eye filming the trash compactor scene in A New Hope.

(He quickly recovered!)

In its earliest form, *Star Wars* **didn't begin "a long time ago in a galaxy far, far away...."** **but in "the 33rd century, a period of civil wars in the galaxy."**

THE MILK FROM A BANTHA IS BLUE.

Animatronic tauntauns in *The Empire Strikes Back* had tubes pumping air in their nostrils to make their breathing appear natural.

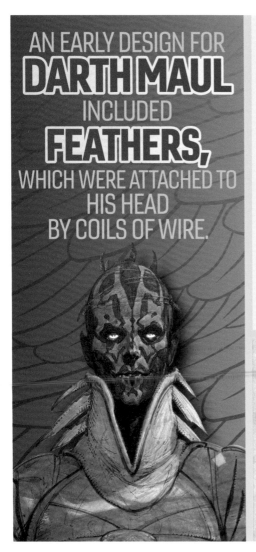

AN EARLY DESIGN FOR
DARTH MAUL
INCLUDED
FEATHERS,
WHICH WERE ATTACHED TO
HIS HEAD
BY COILS OF WIRE.

In 2021, a Disneyland Resort hotel displayed an **edible model** of **Black Spire Outpost** and the **Millennium Falcon.**

The numeral **1138** appears in many Star Wars productions as a nod to George Lucas's first feature film, **THX 1138.**

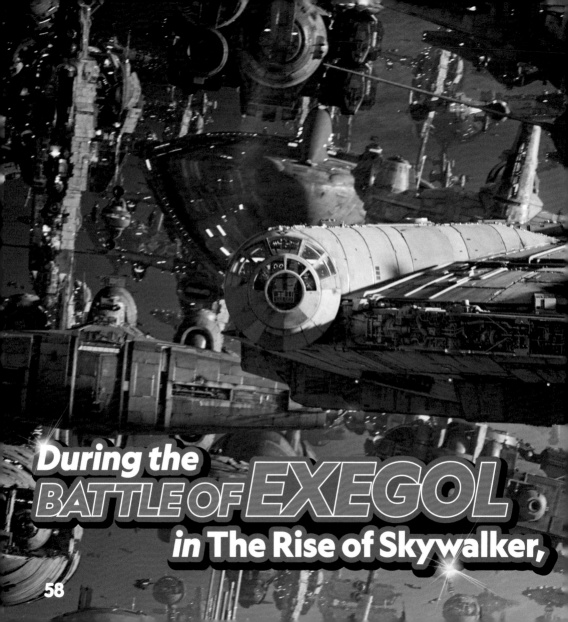

During the BATTLE OF EXEGOL in The Rise of Skywalker,

14,448

SHIPS *come to the* AID OF THE REBELS.

A **PET** in *Star Wars Resistance* was a creature originally designed **20 YEARS** earlier for *The Phantom Menace*.

Mark Hamill has voiced other *Star Wars* characters including **BOOLIO** in *The Rise of Skywalker* and **EV-9D9** in *The Mandalorian*.

Jar Jar Binks was originally going to have **green-colored skin.**

ANAKIN SKYWALKER'S PODRACER WAS INSPIRED BY ITALIAN RACE CARS

THAT GEORGE LUCAS LIKED.

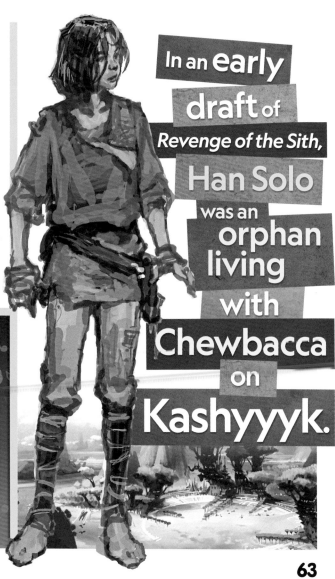

The **slimy sound** of *Jabba the Hutt's* **movements** was made mainly with recordings of hands being run through a bowl of **macaroni** and **cheese.**

The opening notes of *The Mandalorian's* **theme song** were played on a bass recorder —an instrument similar to recorders students play in school.

In an **early draft** of *Revenge of the Sith,* **Han Solo** was an **orphan living** with **Chewbacca** on **Kashyyyk.**

63

Twelve of the **JAWAS** in *A New Hope* were played by **LOCAL TUNISIAN CHILDREN.**

George Lucas finished *A New Hope* less than two weeks before it opened in theaters.

In Disney Parks' *Star Wars: Galaxy's Edge*®
there are **tracks** in the pathways made
from the original

R2-D2
droid.

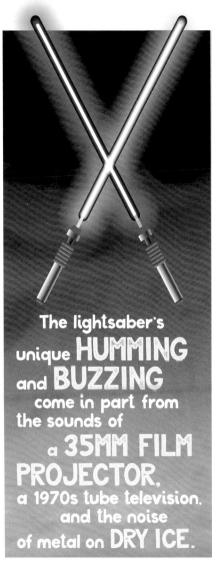

The lightsaber's unique **HUMMING** and **BUZZING** come in part from the sounds of **a 35MM FILM PROJECTOR**, a 1970s tube television, and the noise of metal on **DRY ICE**.

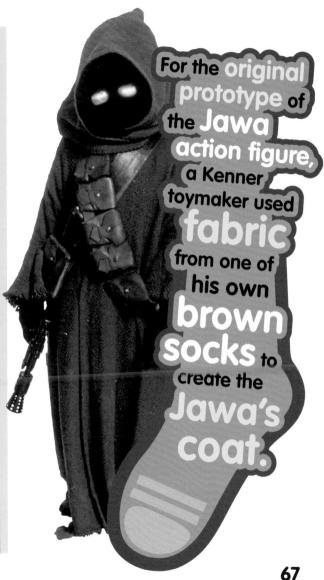

For the original prototype of the **Jawa** action figure, a Kenner toymaker used **fabric** from one of his own **brown socks** to create the **Jawa's coat.**

THE CREATOR OF THE **RANCOR** IN *RETURN OF THE JEDI* DESCRIBED

SEVEN MILLION POUNDS (3.2 MILLION KG)

THE **CREATURE** AS A CROSS BETWEEN A **BEAR** AND A **POTATO.**

OF SNOW WERE USED TO CREATE A *STAR WARS* SCULPTURE IN JAPAN THAT INCLUDED DARTH VADER AND THE DEATH STAR.

DURING THE **DESIGN PROCESS** FOR *THE FORCE AWAKENS,* **BB-8'S** NICKNAME WAS **"SURLY."**

It took **FOUR CREW MEMBERS** *to* **LIFT KLAUD'S HEAD** *onto his body while filming* **The Rise of Skywalker.**

The design for **COUNT DOOKU'S LIGHTSABER HANDLE** in *Attack of the Clones* was based partially on a Filipino weapon called a **BARONG.**

FRITO–LAY RELEASED **TWISTED CHEETOS** SNACKS THAT WERE "**DARTH VADER DARK**" AND "YODA GREEN" FOR THE RELEASE OF **REVENGE OF THE SITH.**

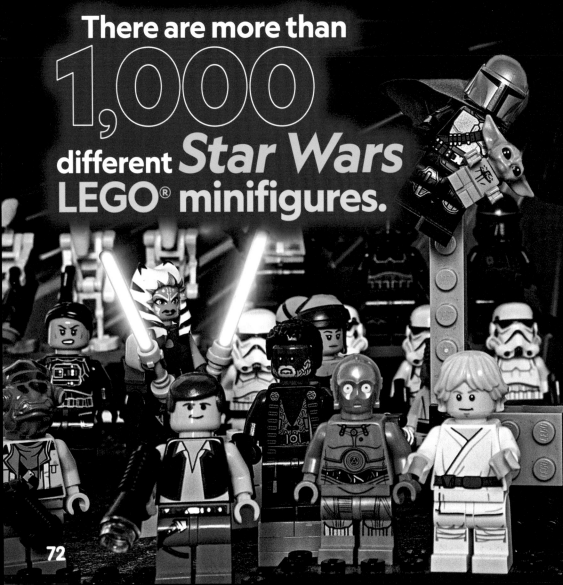

There are more than
1,000
different *Star Wars*
LEGO® minifigures.

The **Jar Jar Binks** minifigure included the **first unique head shape** for a **LEGO®** figure.

73

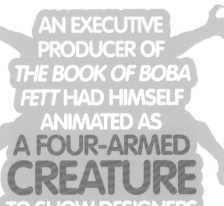

AN EXECUTIVE PRODUCER OF *THE BOOK OF BOBA FETT* HAD HIMSELF ANIMATED AS A FOUR-ARMED **CREATURE** TO SHOW DESIGNERS HIS VISION OF THE TATOOINE SAND BEAST.

The facial expressions of **Rogue One's** *Admiral Raddus* are based on those of former **British** prime minister **WINSTON CHURCHILL.**

THE DARTH VADER **COSTUME USED** IN *OBI-WAN KENOBI* WAS SO **HOT** TO **WEAR** THAT IT INCLUDED A **COOLING SYSTEM.**

PEOPLE WALKED ON **EGGS** AND SLABS OF **BEEF FAT** TO MIMIC THE SOUND OF WALKING THROUGH **A SPACE SLUG** IN *THE EMPIRE STRIKES BACK.*

VISITORS AT **DOK-ONDAR'S DEN OF ANTIQUITIES** IN DISNEY'S *STAR WARS: GALAXY'S EDGE*® CAN SEE AN ANIMATRONIC **BABY SARLACC.**

THE MODEL FOR
THE DEATH STAR TRENCH RUN
IN A NEW HOPE WAS
SET UP IN THE PARKING LOT
OF INDUSTRIAL LIGHT & MAGIC.

THE DEATH STAR TRENCH
CONSTRUCTED FOR
THE BATTLE OF YAVIN WAS
60 FEET (18 M) LONG—
LONGER THAN
A BASKETBALL
COURT IS WIDE.

IT TOOK MORE THAN
70 HOURS OF
STOP-MOTION FILMING TO CREATE THE
40-SECOND
DEATH STAR TRENCH RUN
ANIMATION.

Industrial Light & Magic is the visual effects company founded by George Lucas in 1975.

ACTOR ALAN TUDYK WORE **STILTS** IN SOME SCENES WHERE HE PORTRAYED **THE DROID K-2SO** IN *ROGUE ONE.*

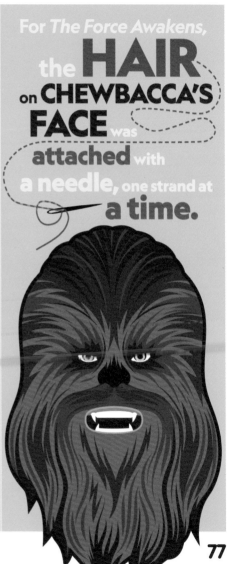

For *The Force Awakens,* the **HAIR** on **CHEWBACCA'S FACE** was **attached** with **a needle,** one strand at **a time.**

77

Different colored COTTON SWABS were used to represent AUDIENCE MEMBERS in wide shots of

The Phantom Menace's PODRACE SCENE.

78

YODA LIVES TO BE **900** YEARS OLD

—THAT'S MORE THAN NINE TIMES OLDER THAN MOST TORTOISES.

The heads of assassin droids **IG-11** and **IG-88** were made from World War II **JET-ENGINE FLAME CANISTERS.**

THE DRENGIR PLANT CREATURES IN THE HIGH REPUBLIC SERIES **EAT MEAT,** JUST LIKE CARNIVOROUS PLANTS ON EARTH.

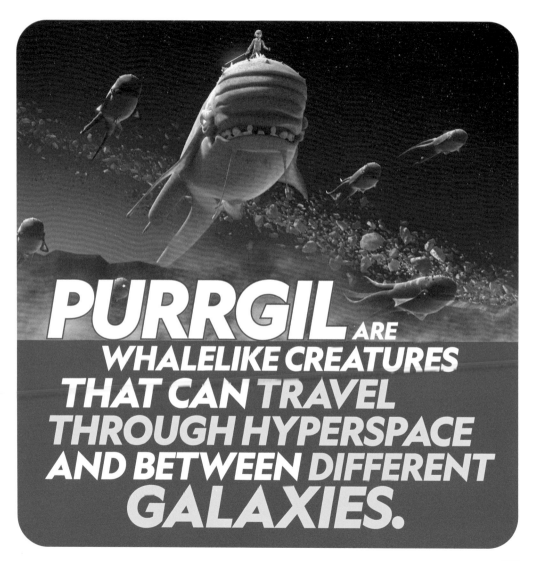

PURRGIL *ARE* **WHALELIKE CREATURES THAT CAN TRAVEL THROUGH HYPERSPACE AND BETWEEN DIFFERENT GALAXIES.**

AUNT Z in *Star Wars Resistance* has a **TATTOO** of a **SPACE WAFFLE** on her arm.

The original *Star Wars* film was not referred to as *A New Hope* until the film was rereleased in theaters in 1981, **four years after it had premiered.**

It was also at that time that it was first labeled *Episode IV.*

BOBA FETT

SHARES THE SAME GENETIC PATTERN AS HIS FATHER,

JANGO FETT,

MAKING HIM JANGO'S **TWIN**

AS WELL AS HIS ADOPTED SON.

Wookiees speak three different languages: Shyriiwook, Thykarann, and Xaczik (but understand many more!).

THE SHAPE OF **MICKEY MOUSE'S HEAD** AND **EARS** BRIEFLY APPEARS IN CLOUD CITY IN *THE EMPIRE STRIKES BACK.*

After Carrie Fisher as Leia says **"I love you"** to Han Solo in *The Empire Strikes Back,* actor Harrison Ford says **"I know,"** which was not in the script.

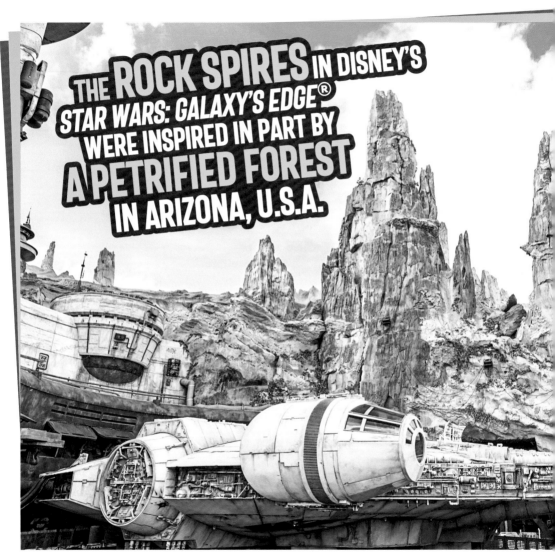

THE **ROCK SPIRES** IN DISNEY'S *STAR WARS: GALAXY'S EDGE®* WERE INSPIRED IN PART BY A **PETRIFIED FOREST** IN ARIZONA, U.S.A.

An actor inside **R2-D2** played the droid in some *Star Wars* scenes—in other scenes the droid was **REMOTE-CONTROLLED** or **COMPUTER-GENERATED.**

BEEP BOOP!

TO MAINTAIN SECRECY ON STAR WARS FILMS AND TV SERIES, THESE PROJECT CODE NAMES WERE USED:

-ILM-
BLUE HARVEST
JP-011B   5-14-82
115-43B   1   TOMBLIN
PLATE #   GLENNON
563   VV-3

BLUE HARVEST
(Return of the Jedi)

LOS ALAMOS
(Rogue One)

AVCO
(The Force Awakens)

PROJECT HUCKLEBERRY
(The Mandalorian)

SPACE BEAR
(The Last Jedi)

TRIXIE
(The Rise of Skywalker)

RED CUP
(Solo)

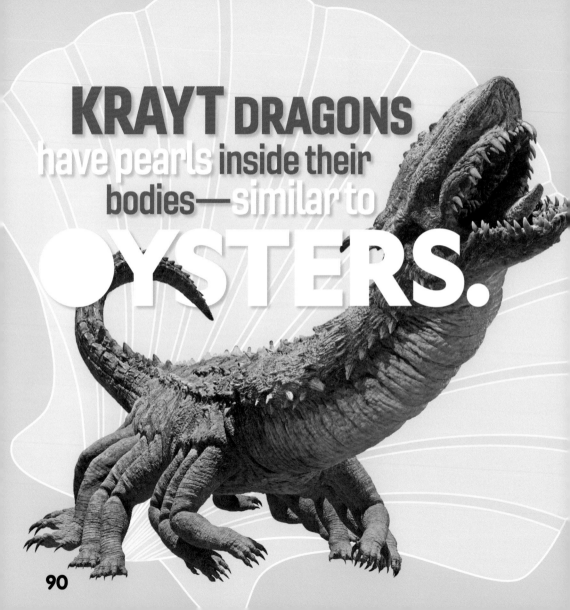

KRAYT DRAGONS have pearls inside their bodies—similar to OYSTERS.

MACE WINDU was the first **on-screen** character to have **A PURPLE LIGHTSABER.**

BIRD RECORDINGS AND A TURKEY CALL WERE USED TO MAKE THE PORG NOISES HEARD IN *THE LAST JEDI.*

George Lucas used aerial combat scenes from old war movies to help visual effects artists create battle shots for A New Hope.

Garazeb "Zeb" Orrelios in *Star Wars Rebels* was designed as a cross between the original concept art for Chewbacca and a cat.

 "WEIRD AL" YANKOVIC sings about how Anakin "may be Vader someday later" to the tune of "American Pie" in the *Star Wars* parody song **"THE SAGA BEGINS."**

The **AZUMEL ALIEN** species has **SIX EYES,** as do spitting spiders on Earth.

93

were not going to be siblings.

95

THE SOUNDS OF
BOGA,
A FEMALE VARACTYL,
IN *REVENGE OF THE SITH*
WERE MADE FROM
RECORDINGS OF
DOGS, COYOTES, AND
A TASMANIAN DEVIL.

An **EARLY IDEA** for **YODA** involved using a **TRAINED MONKEY** instead of **A PUPPET.**

The sound designer for *A New Hope* considered creating **a sound** for Darth Vader's **heartbeat.**

SOUNDS FROM A **MICROPHONE** INSIDE A **SCUBA MASK** WERE USED TO **CREATE** THE SOUNDS OF **DARTH VADER BREATHING.**

That's weird!

MATTEL TESTED MORE THAN **80** SETS OF **EYES** FOR ONE OF ITS GROGU **TOYS.**

More than
400 people
were cast as extras
to play the **Aki-Aki** on **Pasaana**
in *The Rise of Skywalker*—including
soldiers from
the **Jordanian army.**

101

The **GHOST** ship

from the animated series

STAR WARS REBELS

made its first **LIVE-ACTION APPEARANCE** in the film *Rogue One.*

SOME INTERGALACTIC LANGUAGES—LIKE **HUTTESE,** SPOKEN BY JABBA THE HUTT— ARE **BASED** ON **REAL LANGUAGES.**

A PREHISTORIC RHINOCEROS WAS AN **INSPIRATION** FOR THE **MUDHORN** IN THE MANDALORIAN.

That's weird!

Visual effects artists studied large animals hunting prey to create the motion of the **AT-AT WALKERS** in *The Empire Strikes Back.*

Trash cans in Disney's *Star Wars: Galaxy's Edge*® include the number **3263827**—the trash compactor hatch number Luke gets trapped inside in *A New Hope*.

Star Wars *fans can get married* at the same Italian villa *where **Anakin** and **Padmé's** wedding was **filmed** for* Attack of the Clones.

I do!

The Corellian hounds in *Solo* were played by dogs wearing costumes.

The nickname "Buckets of Blood" for Jedi Master Torban Buck from The High Republic was inspired by an actual New York City medic who went by the same nickname.

In **1981,** George Lucas sold the rights to **adapt** *Star Wars* into a radio drama for **one dollar** to the University of Southern California, **his alma mater.**

A LIFE-SIZE STATUE OF

YODA
GREETS GUESTS VISITING LUCASFILM'S HEADQUARTERS
in San Francisco, California.

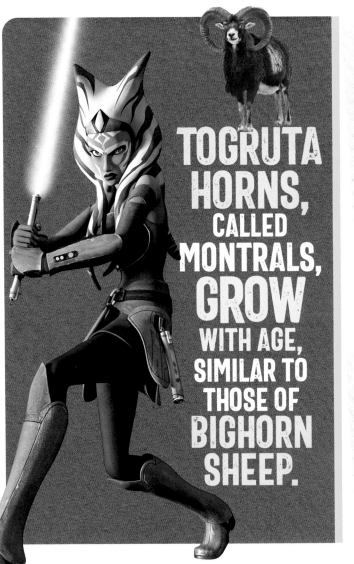

TOGRUTA HORNS, CALLED MONTRALS, GROW WITH AGE, SIMILAR TO THOSE OF BIGHORN SHEEP.

When the **first draft** of *Star Wars* reached more than **200 pages** long,

— George Lucas realized the **project** would need to be **split into three parts,**

which became the **original trilogy.**

THE CHARACTER OF NUBS IN YOUNG JEDI ADVENTURES WAS INSPIRED BY THE SHOWRUNNER'S WISH TO SEE A BLUE TEDDY BEAR SWINGING A LIGHTSABER.

NUBS WAS NAMED AFTER THE SHOWRUNNER'S FAMILY DOG.

THE KENARI LANGUAGE IN ANDOR IS A BLEND OF PORTUGUESE, SPANISH, AND MAGYAR.

TUNISIA, a country in northern Africa, had its FIRST WINTER RAINSTORM in 50 YEARS during the first week of filming Star Wars.

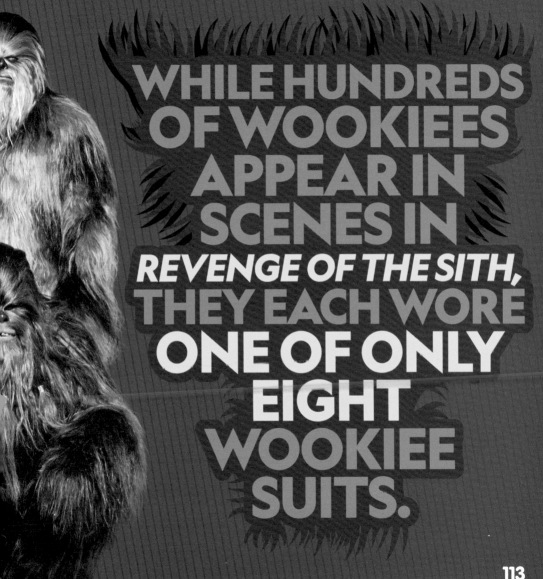

WHILE HUNDREDS OF WOOKIEES APPEAR IN SCENES IN *REVENGE OF THE SITH,* THEY EACH WORE ONE OF ONLY EIGHT WOOKIEE SUITS.

After a **MALFUNCTION WITH THE MECHANISM** that moved **GREEDO'S MOUTH,** the actor who played him

MOVED HIS LIPS by putting a **CLOTHESPIN** between her teeth.

The Phantom Menace was the first feature film **PROJECTED DIGITALLY** in movie theaters.

Attack of the Clones was the first feature film shot entirely with a **DIGITAL CAMERA.**

NASA scientists nicknamed a dark crater on **PLUTO'S BIGGEST MOON, CHARON,** the **VADER CRATER** after Darth Vader.

They also nicknamed **SKYWALKER CRATER** and **ORGANA CRATER** after **LUKE** and **LEIA.**

THE FACT THAT DARTH VADER IS LUKE SKYWALKER'S FATHER WAS

KEPT OUT

OF THE SCRIPT FOR *THE EMPIRE STRIKES BACK* TO **KEEP THE SECRET SAFE.**

A STAR DESTROYER MODEL USED IN *THE EMPIRE STRIKES BACK* WAS MORE THAN NINE FEET (2.8 M) LONG— THAT'S LONGER THAN CHEWBACCA LYING DOWN.

In the 2020 LEGO® Star Wars Holiday Special, Finn and Rose sing a song to the tune of **"JINGLE BELLS"** in Jabba the Hutt's language—**Huttese.**

MANY *STAR WARS* ACTORS HAVE ACCIDENTALLY MADE

LIGHTSABER **OR**

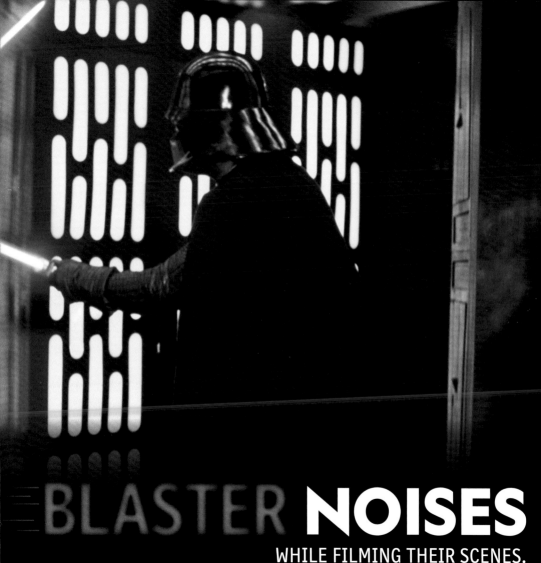

BLASTER **NOISES**

WHILE FILMING THEIR SCENES.

The *High Republic* character **TY YORRICK** was inspired by *Dracula* monster hunter **VAN HELSING.**

The special effects crew's nickname for the nexu in *Attack of the Clones* was "Bad Kitty."

In 1977, empty *Star Wars* boxes with an

"EARLY BIRD CERTIFICATE"

inside were given as gifts—the *Star Wars* action figures weren't available in time for

CHRISTMAS.

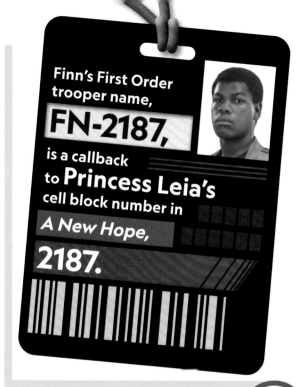

Finn's First Order trooper name, **FN-2187,** is a callback to **Princess Leia's** cell block number in *A New Hope,* **2187.**

Star Wars Rebels animators created **virtual skeletons** for characters to help them **move realistically.**

Strike a pose!

Poe Dameron's

X-WING FIGHTER

from *The Rise of Skywalker*

has been exhibited at the

Smithsonian Institution's
NATIONAL AIR AND SPACE MUSEUM
in Washington, D.C.

PADMÉ AMIDALA'S
NABOO ROYAL CRUISER
IN *ATTACK OF THE CLONES*
WAS MODELED AFTER A
U.S. MILITARY PLANE.

Lupita Nyong'o, who played Maz Kanata, wore **four cameras** attached to her head to capture all of **her facial expressions** while filming *The Force Awakens.*

Oh hey!

The actor who played a **wampa** in *The Empire Strikes Back* stood **11 feet** (3.4 m) **tall** while walking on stilts—that's taller than an **African elephant.**

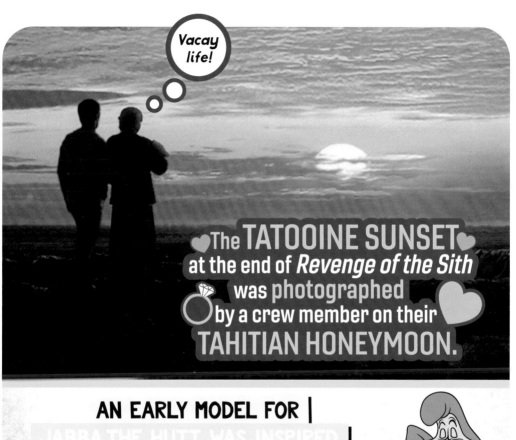

Vacay life!

The **TATOOINE SUNSET** at the end of *Revenge of the Sith* was photographed by a crew member on their **TAHITIAN HONEYMOON.**

AN EARLY MODEL FOR JABBA THE HUTT WAS INSPIRED BY THE CATERPILLAR FROM *ALICE IN WONDERLAND.*

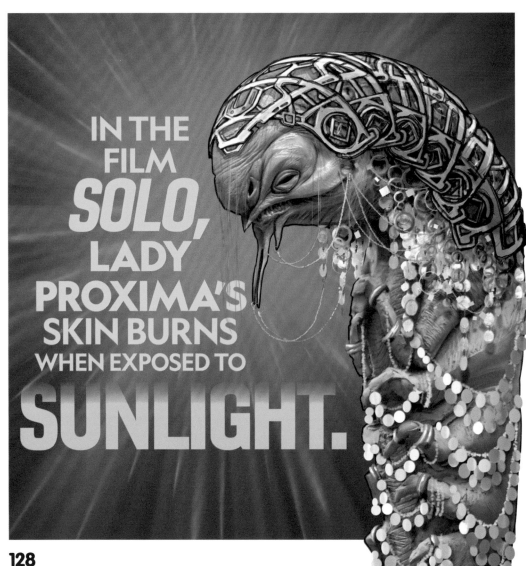

IN THE FILM *SOLO,* LADY PROXIMA'S SKIN BURNS WHEN EXPOSED TO SUNLIGHT.

Billie Lourd, the daughter of **Carrie Fisher,** who played Leia, doubled for a younger version of **the character in** *The Rise of Skywalker.*

LOURD also played Resistance officer **KAYDEL CONNIX** in all three sequel films.

A BACKGROUND CHARACTER NAMED **WILLROW HOOD**

APPEARS TO BE RUNNING THROUGH CLOUD CITY WITH AN **ICE-CREAM MAKER** IN THE EMPIRE STRIKES BACK.

ACTOR
EWAN MCGREGOR
TOLD REPORTERS
THAT HE WAS
GENUINELY
SCARED

THE FIRST TIME
HE FILMED A SCENE WITH
DARTH VADER IN
OBI-WAN KENOBI.

In an **early draft** of *A New Hope*, Han Solo was a **green alien.**

Anthony Daniels, who played **C-3PO,** could not sit down while he was wearing his costume.

THE SOUTH PACIFIC NATION NIUE SELLS *STAR WARS*–THEMED COLLECTIBLE COINS THAT CAN BE USED AS CURRENCY ON THE ISLAND.

CHARACTERS FROM **STAR WARS** AND **THE SIMPSONS** APPEAR IN THE SHORT FILM **"THE FORCE AWAKENS FROM ITS NAP."**

MAGGIE SIMPSON IN
THE FORCE AWAKENS FROM ITS NAP

MATT GROENING

A **bartender** in *The Rise of Skywalker* was played by the Academy Award®–winning composer **JOHN WILLIAMS,** who **wrote the music** for **all nine Skywalker saga films.**

THE GRAND INQUISITOR, a Pau'an, has **TWO STOMACHS—** like alligators and kangaroos do.

In Grover, North Carolina, U.S.A., some residents live on **Darth Maul Drive** and **Yoda Drive.**

The same **SCREAM SOUND EFFECT** can be heard in several *Star Wars* films.

Fennec Shand's
VISOR
in **The Mandalorian**
was inspired by

MEDIEVAL JOUSTING HELMETS.

135

THE **ACKLAY CREATURE** IN *ATTACK OF THE CLONES*
WAS **DESIGNED** AS A CROSS BETWEEN

+

Star Wars films have made more than

A **VELOCIRAPTOR** AND A **PRAYING MANTIS.**

=

$21 BILLION WORLDWIDE.

DARTH MAUL'S cloak was inspired by one a **TIBETAN MONK** wore in a **1940** photograph.

The first model for the **ESCAPE POD** in **A NEW HOPE** was two **PAINT BUCKETS** attached to each other.

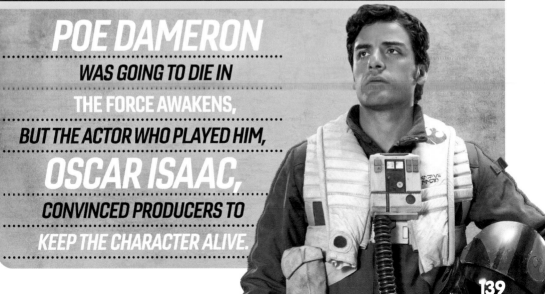

POE DAMERON
WAS GOING TO DIE IN THE FORCE AWAKENS, BUT THE ACTOR WHO PLAYED HIM, **OSCAR ISAAC,** CONVINCED PRODUCERS TO KEEP THE CHARACTER ALIVE.

THE STUNT COORDINATOR
for *Attack of the Clones*
trained **200** people
for the ARENA BATTLE in
GEONOSIS.

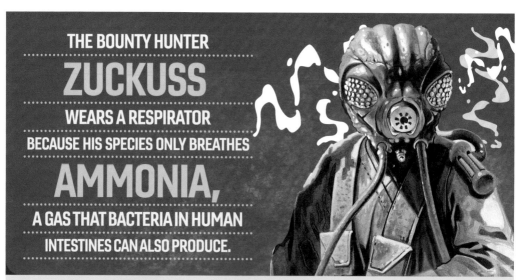

THE BOUNTY HUNTER **ZUCKUSS** WEARS A RESPIRATOR BECAUSE HIS SPECIES ONLY BREATHES **AMMONIA,** A GAS THAT BACTERIA IN HUMAN INTESTINES CAN ALSO PRODUCE.

CREATURE MAKERS USED THE ORIGINAL MOLD FOR YODA TO HELP REPLICATE THE PUPPET FOR THE LAST JEDI.

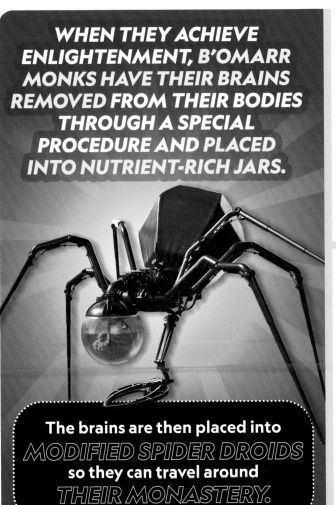

WHEN THEY ACHIEVE ENLIGHTENMENT, B'OMARR MONKS HAVE THEIR BRAINS REMOVED FROM THEIR BODIES THROUGH A SPECIAL PROCEDURE AND PLACED INTO NUTRIENT-RICH JARS.

The brains are then placed into *MODIFIED SPIDER DROIDS* so they can travel around *THEIR MONASTERY.*

Much of *the music heard* in the Star Wars movies was *performed* by the London Symphony Orchestra.

SHREDDED RED PAPER was used to create the planet **CRAIT'S** unique mineral look in *The Last Jedi.*

CAPTAIN PHASMA'S ARMOR is coated with a **REFLECTIVE METAL** salvaged from a **NABOO STARSHIP.**

The actor who played the **REBEL PILOT WEDGE ANTILLES** is the uncle of Obi-Wan Kenobi actor **EWAN MCGREGOR.**

145

Some of **PADMÉ AMIDALA'S** HEADDRESSES WERE SO HEAVY that crew members used a PULLEY SYSTEM TO REMOVE THEM.

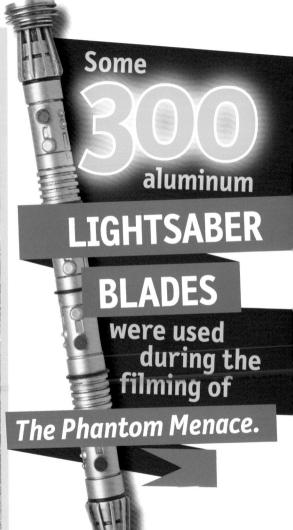

Some **300** aluminum **LIGHTSABER BLADES** were used during the filming of *The Phantom Menace.*

The **HAPPABORE PUPPET** was as long

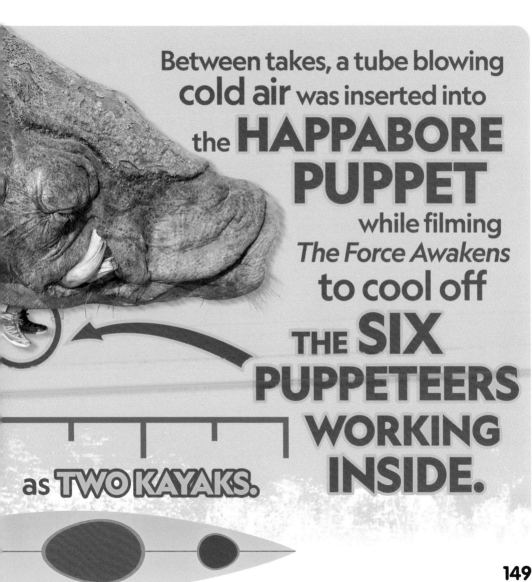

Between takes, a tube blowing **cold air** was inserted into the **HAPPABORE PUPPET** while filming *The Force Awakens* to cool off **THE SIX PUPPETEERS WORKING INSIDE.**

as **TWO KAYAKS.**

The dozens of **CLONE TROOPERS** in *Star Wars* animated projects were **ALL VOICED** by the **SAME ACTOR.**

DR. PERSHING'S costume in *THE MANDALORIAN* is similar to the **IMPERIAL SCIENTISTS'** **UNIFORMS IN** *ROGUE ONE.*

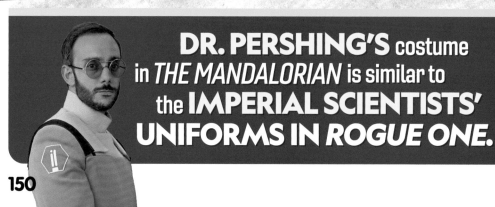

JEDI MASTER KIT FISTO CAN DETECT OTHER PEOPLE'S EMOTIONS WITH HIS TENTACLES.

151

Many of the original **X-WING MODELS** used in A New Hope were destroyed by pyrotechnics, or special effects using fire.

A RARE X-WING MODEL from the film sold at auction for **$2.3 MILLION** in 2022.

THE MENACING TIE FIGHTER SOUNDS WERE MADE BY MIXING SLOWED-DOWN ELEPHANT NOISES WITH THE SOUND OF CARS ON WET PAVEMENT.

CREATURE MAKERS USED THE BODY OF A STUFFED RHINOCEROS TO HELP CREATE THE DEWBACK PUPPET IN *A NEW HOPE.*

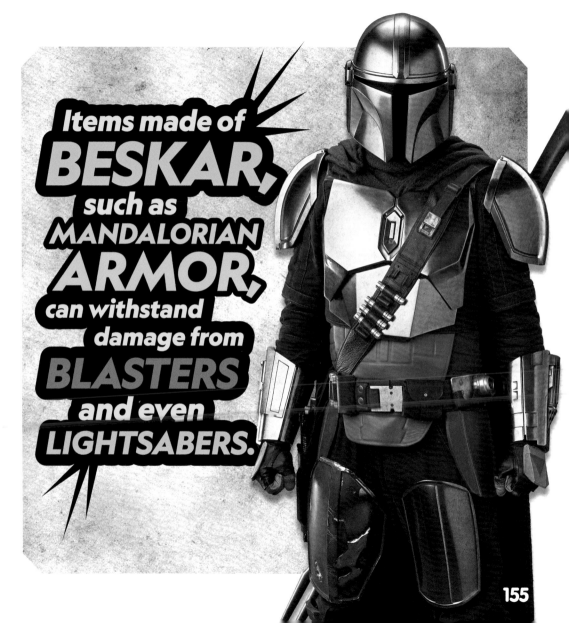

Items made of **BESKAR,** such as **MANDALORIAN ARMOR,** can withstand damage from **BLASTERS** and even **LIGHTSABERS.**

Thank the Maker!

The actor who played C-3PO was the only actor to appear in all nine

SKYWALKER SAGA FILMS.

TO KEEP LUKE SKYWALKER'S APPEARANCE IN *THE MANDALORIAN* A SECRET, ALL CONCEPT ART OF HIS SCENES SWAPPED HIM FOR JEDI MASTER PLO KOON.

THE DROID R3-S6 IN *THE CLONE WARS* IS **BLACK** AND **GOLD** AS A TRIBUTE TO THE **SUPERVISING** DIRECTOR'S FAVORITE **FOOTBALL TEAM,** THE PITTSBURGH STEELERS.

FEMALE TWI'LEKS' ears are shaped like **CONES,** while **MALES** have **HUMANLIKE EARS.**

159

A NEW SPECIES OF

TRAPDOOR SPIDER

WAS NAMED AFTER THE

SARLACC—

A BEAST THAT LIVED IN AN UNDERGROUND LAIR AND

DEVOURED BOBA FETT

IN *RETURN OF THE JEDI.*

STAR WARS
HAS SEVERAL OF ITS OWN ALPHABETS, ONE OF WHICH IS CALLED
AUREBESH.

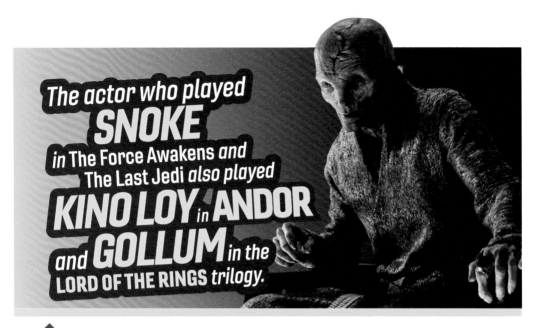

The actor who played **SNOKE** in The Force Awakens and The Last Jedi *also played* **KINO LOY** *in* **ANDOR** *and* **GOLLUM** in the LORD OF THE RINGS *trilogy.*

A Star Destroyer set built for *The Rise of Skywalker* **was as tall as a four-story building.**

A BATTLE SCENE WITH RESISTANCE FIGHTERS RIDING ORBAKS WAS FILMED ON THE STAR DESTROYER SET USING 30 HORSES.

161

Creature designers had to make the **KRAYT DRAGON'S MOUTH** in *The Mandalorian* **BIG ENOUGH** to **SWALLOW** an **EIGHT-FOOT** (2.4-m)-**TALL BANTHA.**

JAMES BOND ACTOR **DANIEL CRAIG** PLAYED A **FIRST ORDER STORMTROOPER** IN THE FORCE AWAKENS.

THE FILM CREW GAVE **CRAIG'S** FIRST ORDER **TROOPER** THE NICKNAME **FN-007,** AFTER THE FAMOUS **SPY'S 007** DESIGNATION.

STUDIO EXECUTIVES *WERE* **CONCERNED** THAT **CHEWBACCA** WASN'T *WEARING ANY CLOTHING* DURING THE FILMING OF A NEW HOPE.

GENERAL LEIA ORGANA'S APPEARANCE
IN *THE RISE OF SKYWALKER* CAME FROM UNUSED
FOOTAGE FROM *THE FORCE AWAKENS*.

GEORGE LUCAS
CAME UP WITH THE IDEA
OF THE GEONOSIANS
WHILE HIS HOUSE HAD
A TERMITE INFESTATION.

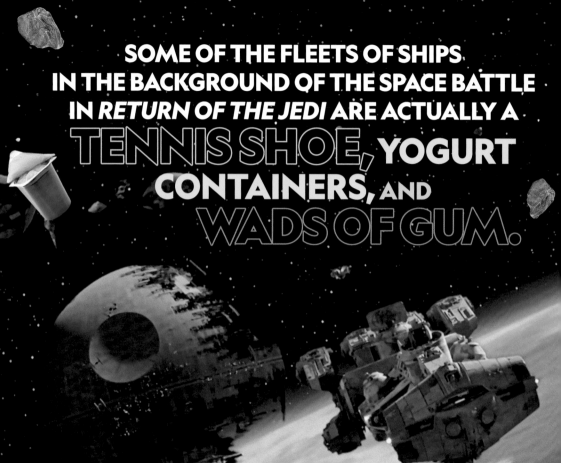

SOME OF THE FLEETS OF SHIPS IN THE BACKGROUND OF THE SPACE BATTLE IN *RETURN OF THE JEDI* ARE ACTUALLY A TENNIS SHOE, YOGURT CONTAINERS, AND WADS OF GUM.

Geonosians, like honeybees, have a **queen** of their **hive**.

EARLY CONCEPT ART for *A New Hope* included an **ILLUSTRATION** of a **STORMTROOPER HOLDING** a **LIGHTSABER.**

FOUR TONS (3.6 t) of **CLAY** were used to **CONSTRUCT** the **JABBA THE HUTT** puppet for *Return of the Jedi*— that's the **WEIGHT** of **AN ADULT HIPPOPOTAMUS.**

CARRIE FISHER'S DOG **GARY** INSPIRED the **ANIMATRONIC ALIEN DOG** SEEN IN THE CANTO BIGHT CASINO IN *THE LAST JEDI.*

171

The **helmet designs** for **jet troopers** in *The Rise of Skywalker* were **inspired** by spider mandibles.

PARTS OF *ROGUE ONE* WERE **FILMED IN**
A LONDON SUBWAY STATION
IN THE **MIDDLE OF THE NIGHT** BEFORE THE MORNING RUSH HOUR.

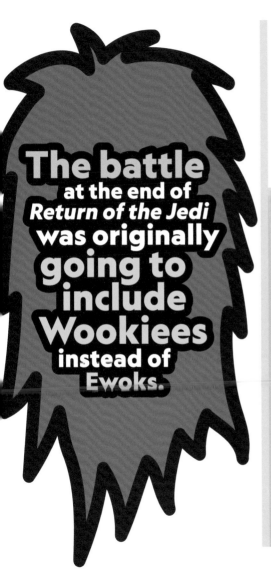

The battle at the end of *Return of the Jedi* was originally going to include Wookiees instead of Ewoks.

THE THREE FILM TRILOGIES KNOWN AS THE SKYWALKER SAGA RUN 1,226 MINUTES, OR 73,560 SECONDS.

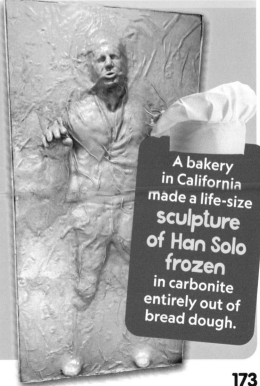

A bakery in California made a life-size **sculpture** of Han Solo **frozen** in carbonite entirely out of bread dough.

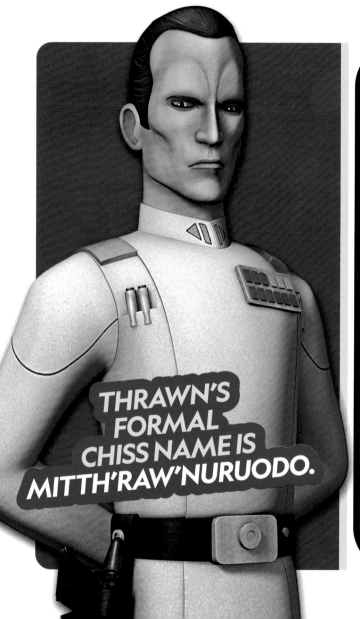

THRAWN'S FORMAL CHISS NAME IS MITTH'RAW'NURUODO.

GEODE, A MALE OF THE **VINTIAN** *STAR WARS* SPECIES, COULD BE MISTAKEN **FOR A LARGE ROCK.**

GEODE'S **TRUE NAME** CAN BE SAID **OUT LOUD** ONLY BY SPECIES THAT **DO NOT HAVE A MOUTH.**

THE **LIGHTING** IN THE **ECHO BASE** AND **HOTH SCENES** IN *THE EMPIRE STRIKES BACK* **MAY BE WHY SOME PEOPLE THINK HAN SOLO'S BROWN PARKA** IS **BLUE.**

A stack of **DIRTY DISHES** helped inspire the **SHAPE OF THE MILLENNIUM FALCON.**

JAXXON, of the *Star Wars* **ALIEN SPECIES LEPI,** looks **VERY SIMILAR** to a **LARGE GREEN RABBIT.**

The creator of the **MON CALAMARI** species named it after his lunch one day—a **CALAMARI SALAD.**

This aquatic species' **SKIN FADES** in color **WITH AGE—** similar to that of **BETTA FISH.**

Din Djarin's **"WHISTLING BIRDS"** weapon in *The Mandalorian* was **INSPIRED BY FIREWORKS.**

GEONOSIAN BRAIN WORMS can TAKE OVER their HOSTS, similar to the way some PARASITES ON EARTH can TAKE OVER the MINDS of ants.

177

The **DARTH VADER VERSION** of **MR. POTATO HEAD** is named **DARTH TATER.**

Some of the ASTEROIDS in *THE EMPIRE STRIKES BACK* **ARE ACTUALLY POTATOES.**

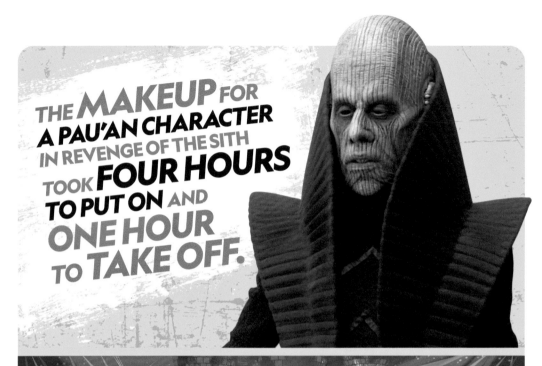

THE **MAKEUP** FOR A PAU'AN CHARACTER IN REVENGE OF THE SITH TOOK **FOUR HOURS** TO PUT ON AND **ONE HOUR** TO **TAKE OFF.**

A DISCO VERSION OF THE *STAR WARS* THEME WAS A **NUMBER ONE SONG** ON THE POPULAR BILLBOARD **HOT 100** IN **1977.**

A COSTUME DESIGNER USED A **VINTAGE ITALIAN BEDSPREAD** TO MAKE THE **WEDDING DRESS** PADMÉ AMIDALA **WEARS** IN ATTACK OF THE CLONES.

181

A NEW HOPE was the FIRST MAJOR FILM TRANSLATED into the NAVAJO LANGUAGE.

The **BLUE** AND **GREEN MILKS** sold at the Milk Stand in Disney's *Star Wars: Galaxy's Edge®* **ARE NOT MADE FROM COW'S MILK.**

They're **MADE FROM COCONUT AND RICE MILKS WITH ADDED FLAVORS** such as dragon fruit and orange blossom.

A CHAMPION RACE CAR DRIVER *PERFORMED DRIVING STUNTS* IN SOLO.

JABBA THE HUTT'S SON, ROTTA, IS NICKNAMED Stinky.

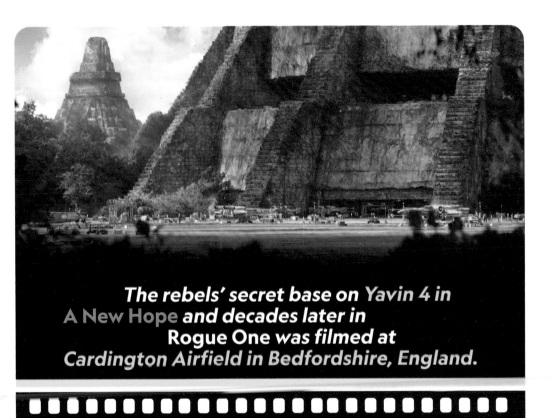

The rebels' secret base on Yavin 4 in A New Hope and decades later in Rogue One was filmed at Cardington Airfield in Bedfordshire, England.

THE TRAILER FOR *THE RISE OF SKYWALKER* WAS VIEWED MORE THAN 111 MILLION TIMES IN 24 HOURS.

SCENES SET ON THE WATERY PLANET AHCH-TO IN *THE LAST JEDI* WERE FILMED ON A REMOTE IRISH ISLAND THAT IS ACCESSIBLE ONLY DURING THE SUMMER.

THE ANCIENT GAELIC MONASTERY ON THE ISLAND SERVED AS THE REMNANTS OF AN OLD JEDI TEMPLE.

The **THALA-SIREN PUPPET** used in *The Last Jedi* was so **LARGE AND HEAVY** that it had to **BE TRANSPORTED** to its coastal Ireland filming location **BY HELICOPTER.**

SOME
DIGITAL PORGS
IN *THE LAST JEDI* WERE
CREATED TO COVER
UP THE NUMEROUS
PUFFINS ON
THE ISLAND.

187

It took **13 weeks** to construct the **12**-foot (3.7-m) **model** of the **Kashyyyk tree** in *Revenge of the Sith.*

A film camera operating more than **1,000 TIMES** faster than a regular one was used to capture an explosion in *Solo.*

The **miniature model** of Mustafar for *Revenge of the Sith* CONTAINED ENOUGH "LAVA" TO FILL 500 BATHTUBS.

That's weird!

The crust on Mustafar's "lava" included burned cork and kitty litter.

189

THE DROID **K2-B4**
IN *THE CLONE WARS* WAS NAMED FOR
THE BASKETBALL STAR KOBE BRYANT,
WHO WORE THE **NUMBER 24.**

K2-B4 is purple and yellow as a **nod** to the **colors** of the **Los Angeles Lakers**— **Bryant's team**—for members of the crew who were **Lakers fans.**

In **The Phantom Menace,** *the planet* **Coruscant** *is* **covered** *by a* **GIANT CITY.**

Some of its buildings were inspired by **HIGH-RISES** in *New York City.*

ACE SQUADRON PILOT TORRA DOZA has a PLUSH EWOK in HER BEDROOM in an episode of *Star Wars Resistance*.

In *Revenge of the Sith*, George Lucas PLAYED a blue-skinned Pantoran named Baron Papanoida.

C-3PO can interpret more than **SEVEN MILLION** forms of COMMUNICATION—

that's **1,000** times the **7,000 KNOWN** LANGUAGES ON EARTH.

MAYA RUDOLPH, who played the droid **ZO-E3** in Vader Immortal: A Star Wars VR Series, IMPROVISED MANY OF HER LINES.

NORWEGIAN RESCUE SKIERS **PLAYED** SOME OF THE **REBEL TROOPS** IN THE **HOTH BASE SCENES** IN *THE EMPIRE STRIKES BACK.*

A **PLANET** NEAR THE CENTER OF THE MILKY WAY IS **SO COLD** THAT ITS NICKNAME IS **HOTH.**

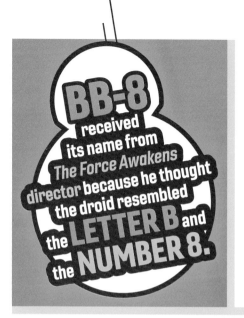

BB-8 received its name from *The Force Awakens* director because he thought the droid resembled the **LETTER B** and the **NUMBER 8.**

SOME VERSION OF "I'VE GOT A BAD FEELING ABOUT THIS" IS SAID IN ALMOST EVERY *STAR WARS* FILM.

In the original edition of *The Empire Strikes Back,* **Emperor Palpatine's eyes** were a combination of the eyes of a **woman** and a **chimpanzee.**

That's weird!

"MAY THE 4TH
BE WITH YOU"
IS A POPULAR
PHRASE
TO CELEBRATE
STAR WARS DAY,
EVERY MAY 4.

FACTFINDER

Page numbers in **bold** indicate illustrations.

206

PHOTO CREDITS

All images © & ™ Lucasfilm Ltd. unless otherwise noted below.

Front and back cover (background), ohishift/Adobe Stock; 1 (background), Aphelleon/Shutterstock; 2-3 (background), Aphelleon/Shutterstock; 4-5, Courtesy of Lucasfilm; 6 (all), Courtesy of Lucasfilm; 7, David James/Lucasfilm; 8, Courtesy of Lucasfilm; 8 (dog), Okssi/Adobe Stock; 11 (UP LE), danielkreissl/Adobe Stock; 11 (UP RT), Courtesy of Lucasfilm; 12 (LE), Irina oxilixo Danilova/Shutterstock; 12 (UP RT), Courtesy of Lucasfilm; 13 (UP), Digital Storm/Shutterstock; 13 (LO), Kuznetsov Alexey/Shutterstock; 14, Courtesy of Lucasfilm; 15 (UP), Courtesy of Lucasfilm; 15 (LO), Courtesy of Lucasfilm; 16 (LE), John Wilson/Lucasfilm; 16 (RT), Lana/Adobe Stock; 18 (LE), François Duhamel/Lucasfilm; 18 (eyebrows), Morphart Creation/Shutterstock; 19 (UP LE), Eric Isselee/Shutterstock; 19 (UP RT), chamnan phanthong/Adobe Stock; 19 (UP background), Nik Merkulov/Shutterstock; 19 (lightsaber), Heritage Auctions, Dallas; 19 (money), Rrraum/Shutterstock; 20, Courtesy of Lucasfilm; 20-21 (LO), Yuliia/Adobe Stock; 23 (yak), Eric Isselee/Shutterstock; 23 (goat), Eric Isselee/Shutterstock; 24 (LE), Courtesy of Lucasfilm; 24 (RT), Courtesy of Lucasfilm; 25 (UP), Courtesy of Lucasfilm; 25 (seal), Johannes Jensás/Adobe Stock; 25 (frame), Peerawit/Shutterstock; 27 (UP RT), Piotr Naskrecki/Minden Pictures; 28 (LE), Courtesy of Lucasfilm; 29, Nicola Goode/Lucasfilm; 30 (UP), Courtesy of Lucasfilm; 31, Courtesy of Lucasfilm; 31 (background), peace_art/Shutterstock; 32 (LE), Jules Heath/Lucasfilm; 32 (RT), Courtesy of Lucasfilm; 32 (background), aekky/Shutterstock; 33 (sink), maksimee/Shutterstock; 33 (UP RT background), ohishiftl/Adobe Stock; 33 (LO), ftomarchio/Adobe Stock; 34 (LE), Courtesy of Lucasfilm; 34 (RT), natrot/Adobe Stock; 35 (LE), natrot/Adobe Stock; 35 (RT), Keith Hamshere/Lucasfilm; 36, Jonathan Olley/Lucasfilm; 37 (UP LE), fim.design/Adobe Stock; 37 (LO LE), Afanasia/Adobe Stock; 37 (RT), Wilfredo Lee/AP Photo; 40 (bear), Justin Horrocks/Getty Images; 40 (vintage microphone), rangizzz/Shutterstock; 40-41 (dolphin), fotomaster/Adobe Stock; 40-41 (background), Ensuper/Shutterstock; 41 (otter), Eric Isselee/Shutterstock; 41 (kitten), Okssi/Shutterstock; 41 (microphone), Fishman64/Shutterstock; 42, Courtesy of Lucasfilm; 43 (LO RT), Justin Lubin/Lucasfilm; 43 (RT background), Ensuper/Shutterstock; 44 (LO RT), Roman Samokhin/Shutterstock; 45 (UP LE), Sue Adler/Lucasfilm; 45 (LO RT), Andrey_Kuzmin/Shutterstock; 46 (RT), Ed Miller/Lucasfilm; 47, Ed Miller/Lucasfilm; 48, Courtesy of The Muppets Studio; 48-49 (glitter stars), Ron Dale/Shutterstock; 50 (LE), Jonathan Olley/Lucasfilm; 50 (RT), Drew Struzan/Lucasfilm; 51 (UP), Courtesy of Lucasfilm; 51 (pencil), Pan Stock/Shutterstock; 52 (RT), Courtesy of Lucasfilm; 53 (LE), janaph/Shutterstock; 53 (LO RT), Courtesy of Lucasfilm; 54 (LO), Courtesy of Lucasfilm; 55, Courtesy of Lucasfilm; 57 (LE background), Gorbash Varvara/Shutterstock; 57 (LO LE), Greg Gawlowski/Iain McCaig/Lucasfilm; 57 (LO RT background), Pupkis/Shutterstock; 58-59, Courtesy of Lucasfilm; 60 (CTR), Courtesy of Lucasfilm; 60 (insets), Greg Gawlowski/Jerryl Whitlatch/Lucasfilm; 61 (UP LE), Melinda Sue Gordon/Lucasfilm; 61 (LO LE), Ed Miller/Lucasfilm; 61 (RT), Courtesy of Lucasfilm; 62 (UP), Heritage Images/Getty Images; 62 (LO), Courtesy of Lucasfilm; 63 (LO LE), dd/Adobe Stock; 63 (LO LE background), Sergey Nivens/Shutterstock; 63 (CTR), Iain McCaig/Lucasfilm; 63 (LO RT background), Ryan Church/Lucasfilm; 65, Courtesy of Lucasfilm; 66 (LO), Gabrielle Biasi/WDI Photographer; 67 (LE), Gorobets/Shutterstock; 67 (LE background), rcfotostock/Adobe Stock; 67 (RT), Courtesy of Lucasfilm; 68-69 (snow), valzan/Shutterstock; 69 (rancor), Terry Chostner/Lucasfilm; 70, Christian Alzmann/Lucasfilm; 71 (UP LE), Ed Miller/Lucasfilm; 71 (RT), Keith Hamshere/Lucasfilm; 72-73, Sarah L. Gardner; 73 (UP), iStock Editorial/Getty Images; 74 (LO LE), Jules Heath/Lucasfilm; 74 (flag), Katsiaryna Pleshakova/Shutterstock; 75 (LO), Sarah L. Gardner; 76, Courtesy of Lucasfilm; 77 (LE), Courtesy of Lucasfilm; 78, Courtesy of Lucasfilm; 79 (LO), Unclesam/Adobe Stock; 79 (RT), François Duhamel/Lucasfilm; 79 (hats), Holiday.Top/Shutterstock; 80 (CTR), Courtesy of Lucasfilm; 80 (LO RT), CathyKeifer/Getty Images; 81, Courtesy of Lucasfilm; 82, Courtesy of Lucasfilm; 85 (UP), Courtesy of Lucasfilm; 86-87, Kaiti Patterson/Walt Disney Imagineering; 87 (RT), Ed Miller/Lucasfilm; 88, Courtesy of Lucasfilm; 89, François Duhamel/Lucasfilm; 90, Courtesy of Lucasfilm; 90 (background), Ganna Bassak/Shutterstock; 91 (UP RT), Ed Miller/Lucasfilm; 91 (LO), Courtesy of Lucasfilm; 92 (UP LE, Ralph McQuarrie/Lucasfilm; 92 (UP RT), Courtesy of Lucasfilm; 93 (LE), Courtesy of Lucasfilm; 93 (RT), Macronatura.es/Adobe Stock; 94, Jerry Vanderstelt/Lucasfilm; 95, Jerry Vanderstelt/Lucasfilm; 96-97, Courtesy of Lucasfilm; 97 (LO LE), tuulijumala/Shutterstock; 97 (LO RT), JulieGaia/Adobe Stock; 99 (LO RT), Javier brosch/Adobe Stock; 100, Willrow Hood/Adobe Stock; 101,

Jonathan Olley/Lucasfilm; 102-103, Courtesy of Lucasfilm; 105 (UP LE background), prapann/Shutterstock; 105 (LE), Courtesy of Lucasfilm; 105 (CTR), Elenarts/Shutterstock; 107 (UP), Sarah L. Gardner; 107 (LO), Willee Cole/Adobe Stock; 107 (LO background), OlgaSha/Shutterstock; 108 (LE), Courtesy of Lucasfilm; 108 (LO RT), Ed Miller/Lucasfilm; 109, Shahana Alam/Lucasfilm; 110 (LE), Courtesy of Lucasfilm; 110 (UP CTR), photomaster/Shutterstock; 111 (RT), Helga Gavrilova/Shutterstock; 112-113, Keith Hamshere/Lucasfilm; 114, Courtesy of Lucasfilm; 115 (background), Johns Hopkins University Applied Physics Laboratory/Southwest Research Institute/NASA; 117, Courtesy of Lucasfilm; 117 (bells), siouxsinner/Shutterstock; 118-119, Courtesy of Lucasfilm; 120, Courtesy of Lucasfilm; 121 (LE), goir/Adobe Stock; 121 (LO RT), Oleg Belov/Shutterstock; 122-123, The Washington Post/Getty Images; 124, Courtesy of Lucasfilm; 124 (LO RT), Stocktrek/Getty Images; 125 (LO LE), Courtesy of Lucasfilm; 125 (RT), David James/Lucasfilm; 126 (LE), Patryk Kosmider/Adobe Stock; 127 (UP), Courtesy of Lucasfilm; 127 (LO background), Nik Merkulov/Shutterstock; 127 (Caterpillar), © Disney; 128, Courtesy of Lucasfilm; 128 (background), Igor Zh/Shutterstock; 129 (LE), Ed Miller/Lucasfilm; 130-131, Matt Kennedy/Lucasfilm; 132 (LO LE), Tartila/Shutterstock; 133 (UP LE), Courtesy of The Simpsons; 133 (UP RT), TM & © 20th Television; 133 (LO background), Francesco Cantone/Shutterstock; 133 (violin), Boiko Y/Shutterstock; 133 (trombone), Dimitriu/Adobe Stock; 133 (saxophone), Mindscape studio/Shutterstock; 134 (Inquisitor), Kevin Estrada/Lucasfilm; 134 (RT background), alphaspirit/Adobe Stock; 135, Courtesy of Lucasfilm; 136 (raptor), Linda Bucklin/Shutterstock; 136-137 (mantis), Ziva_K/Getty Images Plus; 136-137 (money), Rrraum/Shutterstock; 137 (UP), Courtesy of Lucasfilm; 138, Giles Keyte/Lucasfilm; 139 (UP LE), Courtesy of Lucasfilm; 139 (paint buckets), Matis75/Shutterstock; 140-141, Courtesy of Lucasfilm; 142 (UP), Brian Rood/Lucasfilm; 142 (LO), Douglas Dawson/Lucasfilm; 143 (LE), Courtesy of Lucasfilm; 143 (UP RT), Katsiaryna Pleshakova/Shutterstock; 144 (UP), Courtesy of Lucasfilm; 144 (LO), Courtesy of Lucasfilm; 145, Courtesy of Lucasfilm; 146, Keith Hamshere/Lucasfilm; 147, Keith Hamshere/Lucasfilm; 148-149, David James/Lucasfilm; 150 (UP), Courtesy of Lucasfilm; 150 (LO), François Duhame/Lucasfilm; 151, Giles Westley/Lucasfilm; 152 (UP LE), Courtesy of Lucasfilm; 152-153 (background), Courtesy of Lucasfilm; 153 (LE), Courtesy of Lucasfilm; 154 (UP), Courtesy of Lucasfilm; 154 (CTR LE), Luminis/Adobe Stock; 154 (CTR RT), adogslifephoto/Adobe Stock 154 (LO), Courtesy of Lucasfilm; 155, François Duhamel/Lucasfilm; 156, David James/Lucasfilm; 157, Christian Alzmann/Lucasfilm; 158, Courtesy of Lucasfilm; 159 (both), Courtesy of Lucasfilm; 160 (UP LE), Jason Bond; 160 (LO LE), Courtesy of Lucasfilm; 160 (RT), Don Saban/Walt Disney Imagineering; 161 (UP), Courtesy of Lucasfilm; 161 (LO), kwadrat70/Adobe Stock; 162, Doug Chiang/Lucasfilm; 165 (termite background), bamgraphy/Shutterstock; 165 (wood), Yuliya Neshte/Shutterstock; 165 (termite 1), Pan Xunbin/Shutterstock; 165 (termite 2), bejita/Adobe Stock, 165 (termite 3), Leo Blanchette/Shutterstock; 166 (background), Courtesy of Lucasfilm; 166 (gum), Madlen/Shutterstock; 166 (shoe), arka38/Shutterstock; 166 (yogurt), Mara Zemgaliete/Adobe Stock; 167 (LO), Courtesy of Lucasfilm; 167 (honey), COLOA Studio/Shutterstock; 167 (background), Valentyn Volkov/Shutterstock; 167 (bee), nejumi/Shutterstock; 168-169, Ralph McQuarrie/Lucasfilm; 170 (hippo), Emoji Smileys People/Adobe Stock; 170 (scale), WitR/Shutterstock; 171 (mirror), Ingram; 171 (dog), Loic Venance/Getty Images; 171 (RT), Ed Miller/Lucasfilm; 172 (UP RT), JGade/Adobe Stock; 173 (LO RT), MediaNews Group/East Bay Times via Getty Images; 173 (chef hat), Photo Melon/Shutterstock; 174 (UP), Courtesy of Lucasfilm; 174 (RT), LVV/Shutterstock; 175 (UP LE), Chones/Shutterstock; 175 (RT), Sergio Aragonés/Lucasfilm; 176 (background), Romolo Tavani/Adobe Stock; 176 (LE), Ed Miller/Lucasfilm; 176 (menu), Daniela Pelazza/Shutterstock; 176 (calamari), Iryna Pospikh/Shutterstock; 176 (fish), bluehand/Shutterstock; 177 (UP), François Duhamel/Lucasfilm; 177 (LO), Pat Presley/Lucasfilm; 179 (UP LE), Pamela D. Maxwell/Shutterstock; 179 (UP RT), AP Photo/Lisa Poole; 180 (UP), Courtesy of Lucasfilm; 180 (LO), Oxy_gen/Shutterstock; 180 (LO background), Veronika Surovtseva/Shutterstock; 181, Lisa Tomasetti/Lucasfilm; 181 (background), Baleika Tamara/Shutterstock; 183 (UP), David Roark/Disney; 183 (LO), Paul Savulescu/Lucasfilm; 183 (flags), Sunflower/Adobe Stock; 184, Courtesy of Lucasfilm; 186 (RT), Jonathan Olley/Lucasfilm; 186-187, Jonathan Olley/Lucasfilm; 188 (UP), Ryan Church/Lucasfilm; 188 (LO), michal286/Adobe Stock; 189 (UP), Ralf Lehmann/Adobe Stock; 190, Courtesy of Lucasfilm; 191, Lisa Blumenfeld/Getty Images; 192, Courtesy of Lucasfilm; 193, dell/Adobe Stock; 194, Courtesy of Lucasfilm; 195 (RT), Amy Osborne/Getty Images; 196 (LE), NASA, ESA and G. Bacon; 196 (RT), Courtesy of Lucasfilm; 197 (LO RT), Eric Isselée/Shutterstock

Since 1888, the National Geographic Society has funded more than 14,000 research, conservation, education, and storytelling projects around the world. National Geographic Partners distributes a portion of the funds it receives from your purchase to National Geographic Society to support programs including the conservation of animals and their habitats. To learn more, visit natgeo.com/info.

For more information, visit nationalgeographic.com, call 1-877-873-6846, or write to the following address:

National Geographic Partners, LLC
1145 17th Street NW
Washington, DC 20036-4688 U.S.A.

More for kids from National Geographic: natgeokids.com

National Geographic Kids magazine inspires children to explore their world with fun yet educational articles on animals, science, nature, and more. Using fresh storytelling and amazing photography, *Nat Geo Kids* shows kids ages 6 to 14 the fascinating truth about the world—and why they should care. natgeo.com/subscribe

For rights or permissions inquiries, please contact National Geographic Books Subsidiary Rights: bookrights@natgeo.com

Library of Congress Cataloging-in-Publication Data

Names: National Geographic Kids (Firm), issuing body.
Title: Weird but true! Star Wars.
Description: Washington, D.C. : National Geographic Kids, 2024. | Series: Weird but true! | Includes index. | Audience: Ages 8-12 | Audience: Grades 4-6
Identifiers: LCCN 2023030619 | ISBN 9781426375286 (paperback) | ISBN 9781426375354 (library binding)
Subjects: LCSH: Star Wars films--Miscellanea--Juvenile literature.
Classification: LCC PN1995.9.S695 W45 2024 | DDC 791.43/75--dc23/eng/20230706
LC record available at https://lccn.loc.gov/2023030619

The publisher would like to thank the teams that made this book possible:

From National Geographic: Amy Richau, Michelle Harris, Sarah Gardner, and Lisa Bosley, contributing writers; Julide Dengel, leading designer; Gus Tello, designer; Ariane Szu-Tu, editor; Sarah Gardner, Sarah Mock, and Colin Wheeler, photo editors; Lori Epstein, photo manager; Alix Inchausti, production editor; and Lauren Sciortino and David Marvin, associate designers.

From Lucasfilm: Michael Siglain, creative director; Jennifer Pooley, editor; Troy Alders, art director; Leland Chee, senior creative executive; Phil Szostak, creative art manager; Allison Bird, senior photo editor; Bryce Pinkos, manager, photo stills; Chris Argyropoulos, VP, franchise assets & publicity; Elinor De La Torre, archives asset services coordinator; Gabrielle Levenson, director, digital asset management; Michael Trobiani, digital asset coordinator; and Sarah Williams, image archivist.

Printed in Canada
24/FC/2